BATS

NIGHTTIME ANIMALS

Lynn M. Stone

The Rourke Corporation, Inc.
Vero Beach, Florida 32964

Edited by Sandra A. Robinson

PHOTO CREDITS
© Joe McDonald: cover, title page, page 4; © Lynn M. Stone:
pages 7, 8, 10, 13, 17; © James P. Rowan: pages 12, 15, 18, 21

Library of Congress Cataloging-in-Publication Data

Stone, Lynn M.
    Bats / by Lynn M. Stone.
       p. cm. — (Nighttime animals)
    Includes index.
    Summary: Discusses the habitats, physical characteristics, and
behavior of bats and describes some of the different kinds.
    ISBN 0-86593-293-X
    1. Bats—Juvenile literature. [1. Bats.] I. Title.
II. Series: Stone, Lynn M. Nighttime animals.
QL737.C5S745   1993
599.4—dc20   93-1535
                                           CIP

Printed in the USA   AC

TABLE OF CONTENTS

BATS

Bats are furry animals, but they are sometimes mistaken for birds. That is because bats are the only mammals that really fly. Flying squirrels glide through the air, but they don't have wings. Bats flap their wide wings rapidly and fly about like giant moths.

North America's bats are **nocturnal**—creatures of the night. Amazingly, bats "see" not with their eyes, but with their sensitive ears.

Bats are the only furry animals—mammals—in the world that really fly

NIGHT FLIGHT

People may say someone is "blind as a bat"—but bats are not blind. Some of them may see very well. A bat "sees" best, however, by listening!

Flying bats find their way in total darkness by using **echolocation.** Bats make high-pitched sounds. People can't hear them, but the bats can. As the sound strikes an object—perhaps a cave wall or a flying insect—it echoes back to the bat. The bat can tell where the object is by listening to the echo.

For night flight, the bat's ears are much more important than its eyes

HOW BATS LOOK

The Aztecs of old Mexico had a word for bats that meant "butterfly mouse." That is a great description—a dark, furry, bright-eyed little animal with wings.

A bat's wings are made of thin skin that can bend. The wings are attached to its arms, fingers and legs. With wings outstretched, a bat looks like it is wearing a cape.

Bats have a sharp-hooked claw, which they use to hang upside-down. Leaf-nosed bats have an unusual, leaflike growth on their noses.

A sleeping bat at midday hangs upside-down by its sharp-hooked claw in a Missouri cave

WHERE BATS LIVE

Bats live throughout most of the world's land area. They do not live in the coldest places, such as the Far North. They are also missing from some ocean islands.

Most bats are nocturnal. They hunt at night. During the day they rest and sleep in dark places. Tree hollows, caves and building attics are favorite hangouts.

During winter, some **species,** or kinds, of bats slip into the deep sleep called **hibernation.** Others **migrate,** or travel, to warmer areas where they can still find food.

Hibernating little brown bats cluster together for warmth in an Iowa bat cave

The leaflike structure of the dwarf fruit bat, a Latin American species, probably helps the bat's sense of smell

Beads of moisture cling to the fur of a hibernating bat

KINDS OF BATS

People know about nearly 1,000 species of bats. About 40 of them live in the United States and Canada.

The world's largest bats are sometimes called flying foxes. They have wingspreads up to 5 feet and they weigh over 3 pounds. Flying foxes live in parts of Asia, Africa and Australia.

Flying foxes are fruit-eating bats. Other large groups of bats are the fish-eating, insect-eating, flower-feeding, vampire and **carnivorous** bats. Carnivorous bats eat small animals.

An Egyptian fruit bat, one of the "flying foxes"

PREDATORS AND PREY

Most North American bats eat insects. Bats living in other places may feed on fruit, birds, lizards, frogs, fish, flowers and small mammals, including other bats. Flower-feeding bats have long tongues with brushlike tips to gather **pollen** grains from flowers.

Bats are **predators** when they attack and eat other animals. Bats become **prey** when they are eaten. Among the predators that eat bats are some snakes, owls, hawks, eagles and raccoons.

The great horned owl and its night-flying cousins sometimes prey on bats

VAMPIRE BATS

The three species of vampire bats feed only on fresh blood. Their victims are usually burros, goats, sheep, cattle or chickens. People are rarely bitten by vampire bats.

Vampire bats don't kill their prey. The bats only want a drink. The bite, however, can become infected.

A vampire bat looks for a sleeping victim. It settles down quietly and gently. The bat's bite is quick and nearly painless, so the victim in not likely to wake up.

Vampire bats live from Mexico south into South America.

Vampire bats have a gentle bite but a great thirst for blood

BABY BATS

North American bat species raise from one to four young. The mother bat carries her babies as she flies during the first few days of their lives. As the babies grow larger on mother's milk, they become too heavy to carry. Then the mother leaves them at her roost when she flies.

A young bat begins to fly when it is about a month old. In another month, it reaches adult size.

Some species of North American bats live more than 20 years.

Like other mammals, baby bats begin to grow up by nursing on their mother's milk

BATS AND PEOPLE

Bats are generally helpful animals to people because they eat huge amounts of insects.

The story that bats fly into women's hair is often told, but it is untrue. Certain bats, however, have spread the disease **rabies** to people and other animals.

Many bat homes, especially caves, have been disturbed by people. Poisons used to kill insects have destroyed many bats as well.

Thirteen species of bats—six in North America—are **endangered.** They are in danger of disappearing, or becoming **extinct.**

Glossary

carnivorous (kar NIHV or us) — eating only meat

echolocation (EH ko lo KAY shun) — the ability to locate objects using reflected sounds—echoes

endangered (en DANE jerd) — in danger of no longer existing; very rare

extinct (ex TINKT) — the point at which an animal species no longer exists

hibernation (hi ber NAY shun) — the sleeplike state in which certain animals survive winter

migrate (MY grate) — to move some distance from one place to another at the same time each year

nocturnal (nahk TUR nul) — active at night

pollen (PAHL in) — dustlike grains produced by flowers and necessary for flower reproduction

predator (PRED uh tor) — an animal that kills other animals for food

prey (PRAY) — an animal that is hunted for food by another animal

rabies (RAY beez) — a serious disease caused by a virus and spread by bites of certain animals

species (SPEE sheez) — within a group of closely-related living things, one certain kind or type (*little brown* bat)

INDEX